Sea Creatures

Pamela Chanko

Scholastic Inc.
New York • Toronto • London • Auckland • Sydney

Acknowledgments

Science Consultants: Patrick R. Thomas, Ph.D., Bronx Zoo/Wildlife Conservation Park; Glenn Phillips, The New York Botanical Garden

Literacy Specialist: Ada Cordova, District 2, New York City

Design: MKR Design, Inc.

Photo Research: Barbara Scott

Endnotes: Susan Russell

Endnote Illustrations: Craig Spearing

Photographs: Cover: Brian Parker/Tom Stack Assoc.; p. 1, 2, 3 & 4: Norbert Wu Photography; p. 5: Norbert Wu/DRK Photo; p. 6: Norbert Wu Photography; p. 7: M.C. Chamberlain/DRK Photo; p. 8: Norbert Wu Photography; p. 9: Mary Beth Angelo/Photo Researchers; p. 10: Larry Lipsky/DRK Photo; p. 11: Peter Parks/Mo Yung Prod./Norbert Wu Photography; p. 12: Norbert Wu Photograhy.

Library of Congress Cataloging-in-Publication Data
Chanko, Pamela, 1968-
Sea creatures / Pamela Chanko.
p. cm. -- (Science emergent readers)
Includes index.
Summary: Photographs and simple text present the variety of animals that can be found in the ocean.
ISBN 0-590-63880-7 (pbk.: alk. paper)
1. Marine animals--Juvenile literature. [1. Marine animals.]
I. Title.   II. Series.
QL122.2.C48   1998
591.77--dc21   98-23222
                                                                                    CIP AC

24 23 22 21   08   4 5 6 7 8 9/0

Some creatures are long.

Some creatures are fat.

Some creatures are spiny.

Some creatures are flat.

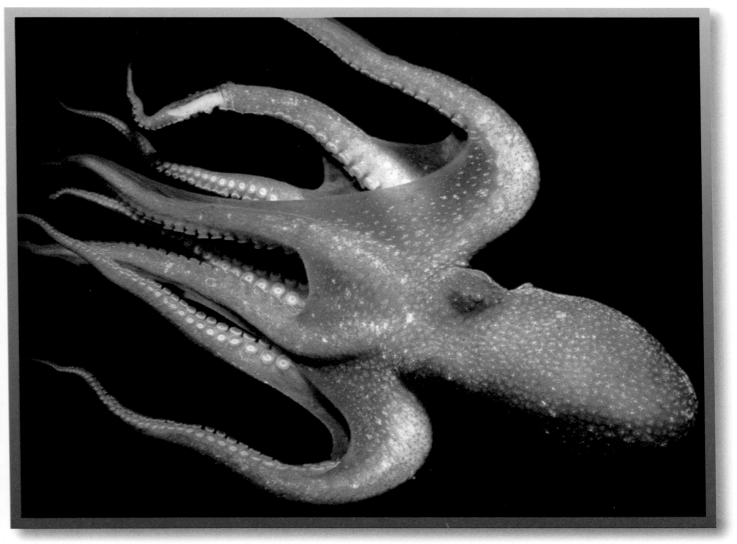

Some have eight arms.

Some have only five.

Some can glide,

and some can dive.

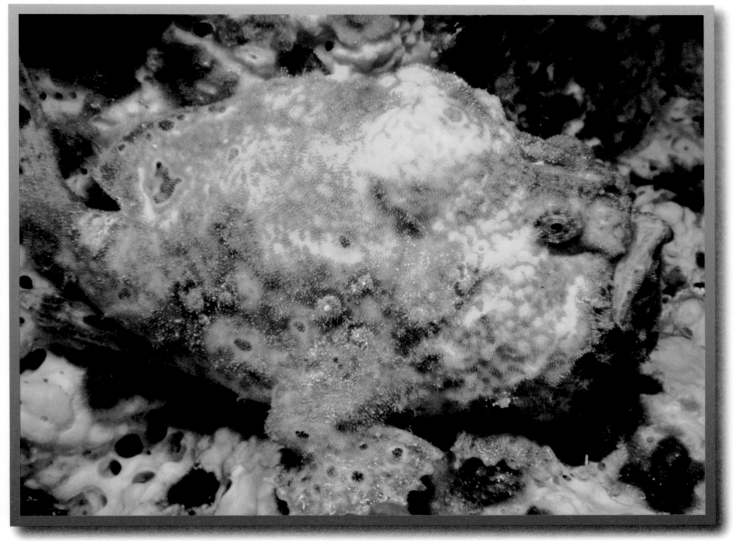

Some are bumpy,

and some are hairy.

Some are bright,

and some are scary!

Sea Creatures

The vast ocean network that covers three quarters of our planet is home to thousands of species of creeping, bumpy, wriggly, slimy, swimming, hairy, scaly sea creatures. Life started in the saltwater of the sea about 600 million years ago. Some of the sea creatures that we see here are among the oldest on earth.

Jellyfish (page 1) have long, sometimes poisonous, tentacles that can extend behind it for yards and yards. They form a stinging trap for the fish that get caught in this network.

The pufferfish (page 2) looks fat, but it is only teasing. When it is frightened it blows itself up to look bigger so that it won't be eaten by larger fish.

The porcupine fish (page 3) uses its prickly spines as a defense against becoming the dinner of another fish. Not too many predators can get past that skin!

The stingray (page 4) is very flat and lies in the sand on the sea floor camouflaged by its shape and color. Its eyes are on top of its head

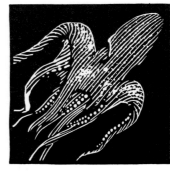

so that it can see from this position, and it keeps its barbed and poisonous tail out and ready to defend itself. The octopus (page 5) doesn't have a backbone but does have eight arms! It can squirt a dark liquid to cloud the water as it swims quickly away in escape from a predator.

Sea stars (page 6), which are often called starfish, have five arms. If one gets cut off or eaten, the sea star can grow another one in its place! The spotted eagle ray (page 7) is from the primitive ray family, which is related to the sharks. It doesn't have either the fins or the torpedo shape of most fish; it glides gracefully through the water as though it were flying.

Whales, like the humpback (page 8), are all expert divers. Because they are mammals, they must regularly come up to the surface to breathe in air through the blowhole at the top of their heads. The bumpy creature (page 9) is the frogfish. Being disguised as a frog is this fish's defense.

The hairy-looking flame scallop (page 10) doesn't really have hair; delicate tentacles wave about in the water helping to draw in the tiny organisms and plankton that it eats. The rhizostone jellyfish (page 11) glows brightly under the water. The jellyfish's body is 98 percent water and it has very little muscle tissue, so it counts on the sea's currents to move it along.

The deep-sea anglerfish (page 12) looks very scary. This fish lives on the sea floor. Its mouth is turned up to catch prey that swim above!